Contents

Detective stories................ 2
Sherlock Holmes................ 3
Spot the detective............. 4
Finding clues.................. 6
Detectives' notes.............. 8
How to be a good detective........... 10
Helping people................ 14
Spot the clues................ 16
Secret messages.............. 18
How to be a good detective: checklist 1 ... 22
How to be a good detective: checklist 2 ... 23
Glossary..................... 24

Detective stories

Do you like detective stories? Detective stories are everywhere! They are on TV. They are in books. They are in films. They are all about famous detectives and clever crimes.

Sherlock Holmes

Do you know about Sherlock Holmes? He was a famous detective who was in a lot of detective stories. He solved a lot of clever crimes. His friend helped him to solve crimes. Do you know what the name of his friend was?

Spot the detective

Can you spot the detective?
Detectives don't wear police uniforms. If they did wear police uniforms, it would be easy to spot them. Detectives don't want people to spot them.

Detectives can work in a lot of places. Some detectives work in shops and stores. They work in stores to stop people taking things. They are called store detectives.

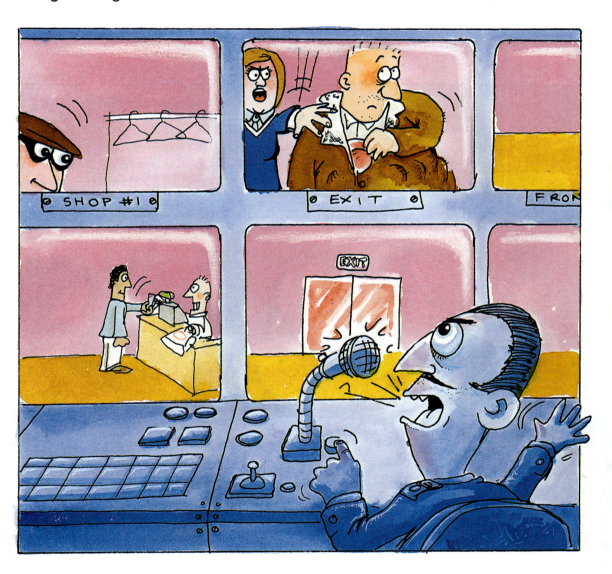

Finding clues

A detective's job can be very hard. Detectives have to solve crimes all the time. They solve crimes by looking for clues. It can be hard to find clues!

Good detectives look carefully at everything. They look carefully so that they do not miss a clue. Every clue is important. If they miss a clue, they may not solve the crime.

Detectives' notes

Good detectives write lots of notes. They write notes to help them solve crimes. They write down what they see. They write down what people tell them.

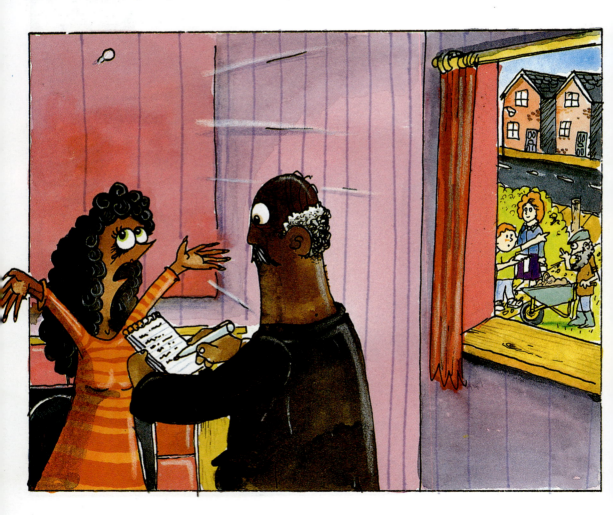

It can take a long time to solve a clever crime. A crime can be a bit like a puzzle. Detectives have to work out all the clues in the puzzle. Then they can solve the crime.

How to be a good detective

Do you want to be a detective? Are you good at spotting things? Do you spot things that other people miss? If you do, then you could be a good detective.

You see a stranger in your street. You want to remember what the stranger looks like. Get out your notebook and pen and write down some notes. The notes will help you to remember what the stranger looks like.

You see a strange car in your street. Write down what kind of car it is. Write down what colour it is. Make a note of the car's number plate. A car's number plate is a really good clue.

If you see something strange, tell a grown-up. Tell the grown-up what you have seen. The grown-up will tell the police.

Helping people

Detectives are good at spotting things. They can spot someone who needs help. Look at this picture. See if you can spot someone who needs help.

Look at this picture carefully. What can you see that tells you that someone needs help? What could you do to help them?

Spot the clues

Are the people who live in this house at home or away? Spot the clues that tell you.

A thief can spot these clues, too! Never give a thief clues that you are away.

Thieves take things that don't belong to them. Thieves often take bikes that don't belong to them. Look at this picture. Can you spot the thief?

Secret messages

Sometimes detectives want to send a secret message. They want their friend to read the message but they don't want anyone else to read it. Do you know how to send a secret message?

To send a secret message you need these things: a white candle, some paper and a pencil.

Get the white candle and the paper. Write a message on the paper with the candle. Write the message in large letters. Can you see the message?

Give the paper to your friend. Tell your friend to rub over the paper with the pencil. As your friend rubs over the paper, the message will appear. Now your friend can read the secret message.

How to be a good detective: checklist 1

Remember! Good detectives…

- Never talk to strangers.
- Never get into a stranger's car.
- Never give clues to thieves.

How to be a good detective: checklist 2

Remember! Good detectives…

- Always look carefully.
- Always write down notes.
- Always tell a grown-up that they know well.
- Always help people.

Glossary

clue   something that helps a detective solve a crime

crime   something that the law says you must not do

detective   a person who finds out things by looking for clues

message   words sent from one person to another person; you can write or tell a message

puzzle   something that is hard to work out; can also be a game

solve   to work out what something means

store   a very large shop

stranger   someone you don't know

thief   a person who takes things that don't belong to them

thieves   more than one thief

uniforms   clothes that people wear to school or work